MODAL**SOLOING**
FORJAZZ**GUITAR**

Practical Strategies For Soloing With Modes Over Must-Know Jazz Standards

TIM**PETTINGALE**

FUNDAMENTAL**CHANGES**

Modal Soloing for Jazz Guitar

Practical Strategies For Soloing With Modes Over Must-Know Jazz Standards

ISBN: 978-1-78933-475-3

Published by **www.fundamental-changes.com**

Copyright © 2025 Tim Pettingale

Edited by Joseph Alexander

www.fundamental-changes.com

Join our free Facebook Community of Cool Musicians

www.facebook.com/groups/fundamentalguitar

Instagram: **FundamentalChanges**

For over 350 Free Guitar Lessons with Videos Check Out

www.fundamental-changes.com

Contents

Introduction

During the mid-to-late 1950s jazz underwent a revolution and a new movement emerged. Musicians who had come through the bebop and hard bop periods – characterized by improvising over complex chord changes with elegance and energy – began to look for a new challenge, and wanted to explore a jazz vocabulary that wasn't constrained by the expected chord progressions.

Modal jazz emerged as the answer to this quest. In this approach to jazz, the key of a tune with its diatonic chords, and the progressions of functional harmony became less important. Those elements were replaced by extended vamps of single chords and shifts between tonal centers that weren't directly related. This meant that musicians now had to focus on using appropriate scales or modes to improvise over the chords, and also find creative ways to keep the music interesting and inventive.

Miles Davis' 1959 *Kind of Blue* album was a landmark album for the modal movement. The tunes *So What* and *Flamenco Sketches* still stand as definitive examples of the birth of modal jazz. They were based around Dorian and Mixolydian modes, and the modes themselves were the point of the compositions.

John Coltrane took modal jazz into more experimental territory with a spiritual intensity. His 1960 recording *My Favorite Things* and 1964 masterpiece *A Love Supreme* were masterclasses in modal improvisation. Other important figures of the era included pianist Bill Evans (who featured on Miles' *Kind of Blue*), Herbie Hancock, Wayne Shorter, McCoy Tyner and George Russell. The latter's book, *The Lydian Chromatic Concept of Tonal Organization* laid the theoretical foundation for modal jazz thinking.

Many of the modal tunes written in the period from the late '50s to mid-1960s still form an important part of the jazz canon and are must-know tunes. In this book, I want to pass on to you a series of strategies for improvising over some of the most popular ones. The book is organized by chord type, so that you can easily transport the ideas to other modal tunes that you want to play.

- In Chapter One we'll tackle Miles' *So What* and Coltrane's *Impressions*. Both tunes use minor chords and have the same two-chord modal progression

- In Chapter Two we'll look at Herbie Hancock's *Chameleon*, a tune based on a minor 7 to dominant 7 ii–V vamp, opening up the possibility of using both minor and dominant modal ideas

- In Chapter Three we'll focus exclusively on dominant 7 chords and look at a range of strategies for playing over them in the context of a modal blues

- In Chapter Four we turn our attention to major 7 and major 7#11 chords working with Freddie Hubbard's tune *Little Sunflower*

- Finally, in Chapter Five we'll dive into ethereal sounding dominant 7sus4 chords exploring Herbie Hancock's *Maiden Voyage*

- In Chapter Six, you have two full-length solos to study that give greater insight into how these techniques can be used in real-world improvisation

By the end of this book, you'll have a range of solid modal soloing approaches to pull out at jazz jam sessions or gigs – ideas that are easy to access and sound good. Plus, you'll have options – from relatively safe, inside-sounding ideas, to concepts currently being employed by the world's cutting edge modern jazz guitarists.

I hope you enjoy the journey and learn some cool new ideas.

Tim.

Modal Jazz Essential Playlist

Miles Davis

So What – Kind of Blue (1959)

Flamenco Sketches – Kind of Blue (1959)

Milestones – Milestones (1958)

John Coltrane

Impressions – Impressions (1963)

My Favorite Things – My Favorite Things (1961)

Acknowledgement – A Love Supreme (1964)

Bill Evans

Peace Piece – Everybody Digs Bill Evans (1958)

Blue in Green – Kind of Blue (1959)

Wayne Shorter

Footprints – Adam's Apple (1966)

Witch Hunt – Speak No Evil (1966)

McCoy Tyner

Passion Dance – The Real McCoy (1967)

Herbie Hancock

Maiden Voyage – Maiden Voyage (1965)

George Russell

Concerto for Billy the Kid – New York, N.Y. (1959)

Get the Audio

The audio files for this book are available to download for free from **www.fundamental-changes.com**. The link is in the top right-hand corner. Click on the Guitar link then simply select this book title from the drop-down menu and follow the instructions to get the audio.

We recommend that you download the files directly to your computer (not to your tablet or phone) and extract them there before adding them to your media library. If you encounter any difficulty, we provide technical support within 24 hours via the contact form.

For over 350 free guitar lessons with videos check out:

www.fundamental-changes.com

Join our free Facebook Community of Cool Musicians

www.facebook.com/groups/fundamentalguitar

Tag us for a share on Instagram: **FundamentalChanges**

Chapter One – Minor Chord Vamps Pt1

Miles Davis' *So What* is perhaps the most well-known and popular modal jazz tune of them all. It features on *Kind of Blue*, one of the greatest, most groundbreaking jazz records of all time, for which Miles brought together a stellar cast of musicians.

The tune has a 32-bar structure and is based on two minor chords (typically played as minor 11s) that modulate up and down in half steps. It starts with sixteen bars of Dm11, then moves up a half step to Ebm7 for eight bars. Then it moves a half step back down to Dm11 for another eight bars.

This means that as the tune goes into its last section and starts over, there are twenty-four straight bars of Dm11 – a fact that has caused many a soloist to lose their place in the form!

John Coltrane's *Impressions* is equally as popular, as it follows the exact same form as *So What*, but played much faster. You can adapt the examples shown in this chapter to fit either tune.

So What and *Impressions* are typically described as Dorian tunes, and the Dorian mode does work perfectly over them, but there are a couple of other strategies we can use to create interesting tensions and melodies.

We'll look at some Dorian ideas first.

Dorian Scale Approach

So What/Impressions begin with a Dm11 chord and were written with a D Dorian tonal center in mind. The D Dorian scale is the second mode of the C Major scale and comprises the notes D, E, F, G, A, B, C. In other words, it's a C Major scale played from the D note.

However, it's better to learn the scale as a sound in its own right, with a D root note. Dorian has a distinctly minor sound and can be thought of as a natural minor scale with a raised 6th degree. That major 6th adds a brighter, more ambiguous sound to its character and stops it from sounding too melancholy.

To get started, here is a question and answer style phrase based on a motif. The major 6th sound is highlighted in bar three.

Example 1a

This line mixes things up a little rhythmically to create interest. For bar one and most of bar two, visualize a regular Dm7 chord voicing in 5th position, with the root note on the fifth string and notice how the scale tones fit around it. At the end of bar two, visualize the top notes of a CMaj7 shape. You'll notice diatonic arpeggios from the key of C Major used from time to time in these lines.

Example 1b

In bar one of this example, play the opening A and C notes with your first and third fingers then quickly shift up into 10th position to continue the lick.

At the end of bar two, we allow an E note to sustain. It's the 9th interval of a D minor chord and implies the underlying harmony is Dm9.

In bar three, the triplet idea can be tricky to play smoothly since it's mostly arranged as two notes per string. The lick ends with an FMaj7 arpeggio shape, which also implies the sound of Dm9.

Example 1c

When working your way through this line, it helps to visualize it moving from a 10th position Dm7 shape down to a 5th position Dm7 shape. It's good to think of your lines being developed around chord shapes. This way you're more likely to play something melodic rather than run up and down a scale pattern.

Example 1d

This example is phrased more like a pentatonic lick. We introduce a chromatic note (C#) into this idea, to approach the D root note from a half step below, which adds a bit of tension and color.

Example 1e

Next we have a scale sequencing idea. When soloing over a single chord for an extended period, we need to get creative with our phrasing. In bars 1-2 sliding articulation on the second string is punctuated with picked notes on the first string. For the first two slides, I suggest using the first finger, then using the second finger for the picked note on the first string, as this gives the notes more separation than barring the top two strings.

When you slide from the 5th to 6th fret, then play the 7th fret of the first string, use your first finger for the slide and third finger for the picked note, then continue this pattern.

You can finger the descending sequence in bars 3-4 however feels comfortable for you, but do use different fingers to play the notes at the same fret on adjacent strings to get a clean, separated sound.

Example 1f

Here is another scale sequence lick. The idea is to play descending scale notes on the top two strings, while ascending the neck. There are lots of ways to construct similar ideas to give your lines momentum and direction. To get out of the sequence, a faster 1/16th note descending run breaks the pattern.

Example 1g

We could spend much more time with the Dorian mode, but I'll leave you to explore its possibilities over the provided backing track. Instead, I want us to move on to a different sound that offers some richer harmonic options: the melodic minor scale.

Melodic Minor Scale Approach

We hinted at the sound of this scale in Example 1e when we played a C# approach note. However, the D Melodic Minor scale contains the notes D, E, F, G, A, B, C#, so here the C note of the D Dorian scale is replaced altogether with the C#. This single change of note creates a new pattern for us to use, and evokes a tenser sound. Check out Example 1h which begins with a typical melodic minor lick.

Example 1h

This line uses an ascending, repeating motif idea. Twice in this line we drop the tense C# note right on the downbeat, which stretches out the tension and resolution. It's good to learn your scales horizontally up the neck on each string, as well as in position. You'll notice that when great jazz guitarists like Martin Taylor take a solo, they often move horizontally across the neck, just using the top three strings.

Example 1i

Here's a line that uses the same principle as the previous example, ascending in leaps on the top string. Notice in bars 1-2 that we're using the same shape, moving up the neck in major 3rds. On their own, these are a series of augmented triads, but played over a D bass note they all become inversions of Dm(Maj7).

Example 1j

Dm11

Example 1k

Dm11

This line is based around minor chord shapes that exist inside the D Melodic Minor scale pattern: first a Dm(Maj7), then a Dm triad at the beginning of bar two, and a Dm(add9) at the end of bar three.

Here's a stretched out scale pattern that starts on the lowest available scale tone on the bottom string. Although this is mostly the notes played sequentially (apart from in bar one, where we omit the B scale note), the fact that we begin low and move across the strings into the top register gives it interest and momentum. It's good to learn your scales this way too!

Example 1l

Dm11

We can use the C# character note of the D Melodic Minor scale in two ways. In bar one, it's used like an approach note to target the D root note from a half step below. In bar two, we lead with the C# on beat 1, which brings out the exotic sound of the scale. In bar three, this short motif uses triads that exist within the scale: D minor, E minor and F augmented.

Example 1m

To end this section, here's a faster lick. Bar one is mostly 1/16th notes played at 110bpm, but look out for the 1/16th note rest at the beginning, so that the line begins a fraction after beat one. Then you'll hold onto the C# for a dotted 1/8th note before resolving to an E at the end of the bar.

Bars 2-3 have an ascending motif. Playing each phrase as a hammer-on and pull-off is the best approach here, both for speed and a fluid legato sound.

Example 1n

Three Pentatonic Scales Approach

When improvising over a static minor chord, many modern jazz players will use an approach that jumps between, or combines, three pentatonic scales. We can work with:

- The pentatonic scale from the root of the chord (in this case D Minor Pentatonic)

- The pentatonic scale a whole step above (in this case E Minor Pentatonic), also known as playing the pentatonic scale from the 9th of the chord (E)

- The pentatonic scale a perfect 5th above (in this case A Minor Pentatonic), i.e., the 5th of the chord (A)

From a theoretical point of view, if we combined the notes of the D Minor, E Minor and A Minor Pentatonic scales we'd end up with a sequence of notes identical to the D Dorian scale. However, the real power of thinking of three separate pentatonic scales is the freedom it gives us to move between the familiar pentatonic box shapes for each scale that we know so well, and each scale adds a unique flavor. Moving from D Minor Pentatonic to E Minor Pentatonic, for example, immediately opens up a different mental fretboard "map" and vocabulary.

To begin with, here are two examples that move from one scale to the next, as indicated on the notation. Listen closely to the different colors each scale creates.

Example 1o

Example 1p

Next, here are two examples that use only the E Minor Pentatonic scale. Imposing the limitation of its five notes on ourselves, we play the B note more often, implying a Dm6/Dm13 sound.

Example 1q

Example 1r

Now, here are two examples using only the A Minor Pentatonic scale. Here, the E note (9th) is featured.

Example 1s

Example 1t

Combined Approaches

To refine your jazz vocabulary and create more sophisticated lines, you can draw on all the ideas you've learned so far and combine them. Example 1u begins with the D Dorian scale, moves into D Melodic Minor, and ends with E Minor Pentatonic.

Play this line slowly and have a close listen to how these different scale colors blend together to create a less predictable melody.

Example 1u

This line begins with 4th intervals from A Minor Pentatonic. The two-note phrasing idea carries over into bar two, but now we're playing 3rd intervals in D Melodic Minor (apart from the 4th interval at the end of the bar). Then we move into a D Dorian phrase, ending on the 6th of the chord.

Example 1v

Here we start the line by descending with the familiar D Minor Pentatonic Shape 1 box. This is quite predictable, but then in bar two we ascend with E Minor Pentatonic Shape 1. The interest is kept up by blending D Melodic Minor and D Dorian in bars 3-4.

Example 1w

Example 1x uses a combination of scales that appeals to my ears: E Minor Pentatonic moving into D Melodic Minor. E Minor Pentatonic over a Dm11 chord has a spacey, open sound, then D Melodic Minor adds the jarring major 7 (C#) over the chord's b7 to create tension.

Example 1x

Lastly, a line that combines three scales all played from the root note. Here we remain in the same tonal center, but focus on highlighting the notes differences between the three scales.

Example 1y

Have fun jamming over the D Dorian backing track in the download and experiment with all the ideas in this chapter.

Chapter Two – Minor Chord Vamps Pt2

In this chapter we look at the minor chord vamp from a different angle. In modal jazz and jazz-funk it's very common for vamps to cycle between the ii and V chords of a key without resolving to the tonic. Herbie Hancock's *Chameleon* is a classic case in point, moving between Bbm7 and Eb7.

Technically, this tune is in the key of Ab Major, but because that chord is never played, Bb Minor feels like the tonal center. Also, although the tune has an overall minor feel, the presence of the dominant 7 chord means that we can build melodic ideas from both minor and dominant scales.

Here are the tools we're going to use to approach this classic modal tune:

- Bb Dorian

- Eb Mixolydian

- Bb Melodic Minor

- The Hybrid Pentatonic approach (Bb Minor 6 Pentatonic scale)

As well as using these scales in their basic forms, in the second half of this chapter we'll push the harmonic boundaries further by using the scales as frameworks, around which we'll add chromatic notes to develop more complex bebop-oriented ideas.

Bb Dorian / Eb Mixolydian Approach

An obvious approach to take when faced with ii and V chords is to play the Dorian mode over the ii and the Mixolydian mode over the V. The Bb Dorian and Eb Mixolydian scales perfectly fit the Bm7 and Eb7 chords of the progression.

These scales contain the same collection of notes, just beginning from different starting points, as they are both modes of the Ab Major scale. In theory, we can therefore focus on just one of the scales and it will work over both chords. Some players prefer to think in terms of minor scales (like Pat Martino), while others prefer a Mixolydian approach (like Robben Ford).

Let's take a listen to how these scales sound over the chords.

Example 2a

Whether you prefer to think "minor" or "dominant", it's good to be aware of the chord you're currently playing over and highlight important chord tones.

This line begins by emphasizing the b7 of the Bm7 chord, then a descending run targets a G note, the 3rd of the Eb7 chord. We immediately drop onto the root of the Eb7 chord to play a partial arpeggio and ascend to target the 9th (C) of Bbm7 at the beginning of bar three. The line ends by playing the 5th (Bb) of the Eb7 chord.

In other words, we've used the scale to improvise, but have done so with an awareness of the effect our note choices have over the chord changes.

Example 2b

I tend to think in minor scales, so I visualized Bb Dorian for most of this line. However, in bar two I played Bb (5th), Db (b7), F (9th) and C (13th) notes on the downbeats to spell a Eb13 chord. In bars 3-4, identical rhythmic phrasing ties together the musical ideas.

Example 2c

If you map the notes of Bb Dorian/Eb Mixolydian across the fretboard, you'll see that AbMaj7 and DbMaj7 shapes exist inside the scales. If we play a DbMaj7 arpeggio over a Bb bass note, as in bar one, this creates a cool Bbm9 sound.

In bar three, the DbMaj7 arpeggio is played again, followed by an AbMaj7 arpeggio in 3rd position. Over the Bb bass note, the AbMaj7 creates a tenser, suspended sound, but it quickly resolves to a chord tone of Eb7.

Example 2d

The next two examples use the Bb Dorian scale as a framework for improvisation, around which passing notes are added.

Example 2e starts with a common bebop note-targeting phrase. It begins with a scale tone (Eb), adds a passing D note, and lands on the Db chord tone (b3) on the down-beat. The D passing note is used again in bar two.

Example 2e

This example places approach notes a half step below Bb Dorian scale tones in bar one, and plays a variation on the D passing note lick in bar two.

Example 2f

Now let's look at some lines using the melodic minor scale over this two-chord vamp.

Bb Melodic Minor Approach

The Bb Melodic Minor scale shares six notes in common with Bb Dorian, but has an A note instead of Ab as its 7th degree. Over a Bbm7 chord this suggests a Bbm(Maj7) sound. In the context of the tune *Chameleon*, when we use this scale over the Eb7 chord it implies a modern sounding Eb7#11 harmony.

Listen to the sound of this scale over both chords by slowly playing this 1/8th note triplet ascending run. The line's repeating motif is adapted for the Eb7 chord and we end on the #11 tension note. This is a useful melodic minor scale sequence you should memorize.

Example 2g

The Bb Melodic Minor scale contains:

- Two minor triads (Bbm, Cm)

- Two major triads (EbMaj, FMaj)

- Two diminished triads (Gdim, Adim)

- One augmented triad (Dbaug)

We can make use of these strong structures, building them into our melodic lines.

This idea leads with two Gdim triads (G, Bb, Db) in bars 1-2. After a scale phrase in bar three, we play an Adim triad (A, C, Eb) followed by another Gdim triad in bar four.

In the context of this tune, the Gdim triad resonates most strongly with the Bbm7 chord, as it contains two of its chord tones. Over the Eb7 chord, the Adim triad contains the root note, while its two other notes are the 13th and #11 of Eb7.

Example 2h

Let's combine the Bbm and Cm triads contained in the Bb Melodic Minor scale and take advantage of the melodic patterns they create across the neck. We can play repeating shape-based ideas, or even think of these notes as a six-note hybrid scale (Bb, C, Db, Eb, F, G).

Bars 1-2 alternate Bbm and Cm triads, while bars 3-4 treat the combined notes of the triads like a scale, descending to land on an Eb root note.

Example 2i

For an even more modern sound, this line combines the hybrid scale notes into a repeating pattern that descends on the top three strings, before transitioning into a scale run. It's worth using a fretboard mapping tool online to help you visualize the pattern of the combined minor triads.

Example 2j

When the Bb Melodic Minor scale is harmonized into triads, chord III is Db Augmented. If that triad is extended to become a 7th chord it becomes DbMaj7#5 (Db, F, A C). The next example uses just the notes of that chord in bars 1-3, and takes advantage of the pattern they create across the fretboard to construct a modern modal lick. The lick ends with a melodic minor scale phrase in bar four.

Example 2k

Let's try this idea again, this time using the notes of Gm7b5 (G, Bb, Db, F), chord vi in the Bb Melodic Minor harmonized scale. For the most part, this line is played in 1/8th note triplets that cut across the 4/4 groove. The lick ends on an F note, the 9th of the Eb7 chord we're playing over at this point.

On your own, try improvising with other four-note chords from the harmonized scale and see which sounds appeal to you.

Example 2l

Learning scales along the length of a single string is a practice advocated by many great players. Box shapes have their advantages, but being able to identify the intervals of a scale on one string across the range of the fretboard opens up the neck in new ways.

This idea uses Bb Melodic Minor scale notes on the top two strings and turns them into a repeating pattern. The line just follows this pattern, regardless of the chords changing underneath and you'll hear in the audio that some note choices sound more tense than others.

One example of this is the A note at the end of the first triplet in bar three, which is played over the Bbm7, creating a tense major 7 over minor 7 sound. However, the subsequent triplet resolves this tension as it lands on a Bb.

Example 2m

Any scale can be used as a skeleton framework, around which we can add passing/approach notes to take things in a more bebop direction. The next group of examples use this idea. Bb Melodic Minor is our framework, but we'll add chromatic movement and target scale tones with approach notes.

This line begins with a descending figure on the top string. Only one chromatic note is added (on the first string, 10th fret) but it's very effective in enhancing the downward momentum. In bar two, this descending motif is typical of Pat Metheny's approach to chromatics.

Example 2n

In bar one of the next line, visualize a Bbm9 barre chord shape in 6th position. This idea targets the chord tones of that shape with approach notes from below. However, we're also using melodic minor scale tones to add more notes on the bottom and top strings to extend the pattern and play a full bar of 1/16th notes.

Example 2o

The melodic minor scale naturally contains some great tension notes, so it only takes a small effort from well-placed chromatic passing notes to fill out a line. In bar one, the chromatic notes are on the third and second strings at the 7th fret.

Example 2p

Here's a line that uses the full range of the neck (but with no chromatic passing notes on this occasion). You'll need to play shift slides with your fretting hand to move fluidly between positions on the fretboard. The slides will be played by either the second or third finger. A slow run through will show you which finger needs to perform the slide on each string.

Example 2q

Here's one more bebop-type line to conclude our melodic minor exploration. This one is inspired by Michael Brecker, who often played long flowing lines, combined with shorter, punchier phrases.

Example 2r

Hybrid Pentatonic Approach

Another approach we can take with modal chord sequences is hybrid pentatonic scales. The central idea behind "hybrid" pentatonic scales is to extract five notes from a parent scale. If the notes are chosen carefully, then it's possible to capture the flavor of the scale while combining it with the playability of pentatonic patterns.

One such useful scale is the Minor 6 Pentatonic scale. I've picked this because it's used by John Scofield and other fusion-oriented players. Here we're using the Bb Minor 6 Pentatonic scale (Bb, Db, Eb, F, G). All of these notes are contained within the Bb Melodic Minor scale. (The same set of notes can be extracted from Bb Dorian too).

Limiting ourselves to these five notes creates a great pentatonic framework for us to work within. The sound of this scale instantly conjures up the wider intervals often heard in Scofield's playing.

It's the G note that distinguishes this minor scale from the natural and harmonic minor scales, and that note is emphasized several times in this first lick. Over the Bbm7 chord, G is the 6th/13th interval. Over Eb7, it's simply the 3rd.

Example 2s

Here's a typical descending pentatonic lick using this hybrid scale. We play a motif in bar one, then adapt it for the Eb7 chord.

Example 2t

Next, here is a bluesy take on the Minor 6 Pentatonic scale, where are bend into its Db and F notes on the top string in a Scofield-esque fashion.

Example 2u

This example begins with an ascending "fours" pattern. We ascend four notes of the scale, return to the second note we played, then ascending four more notes. Then we return to the third note in the pattern, and so on.

In bars 2-4 we play a six-note motif which repeats. Every time the motif is repeated, it is displaced to begin on a different beat, which is a great way of maximizing a phrase over a modal groove.

Example 2v

The main idea of this line is to form short phrases on the top two strings. Using the same rhythmic figure with different notes helps to glue the idea together.

Example 2w

The final example of this chapter begins with intervallic skips, then moves into a motif phrasing idea arranged on the top strings. To finish with a flourish, we deviate from the Minor 6 Pentatonic scale with a fast descending chromatic run, which finishes on the target note of Db, the b7 of the Eb7 chord.

Example 2x

I encourage you to map out the Bb Minor 6 Pentatonic scale across the fretboard and use it to improvise over this chapter's backing track. It's easier to see and engage with the pattern of the scale this way, and it will open the door to you discovering some cool licks.

Chapter Three – Dominant Chord Vamps

In this chapter we'll look at two approaches you can use when tackling blues tunes. You may think that the blues doesn't qualify as obvious material for modal soloing, but it's useful to explore for two good reasons:

1. Like typical modal tunes, the blues gives us long periods of a single chord to solo over, so we can employ modal soloing strategies to create a more modern sound.

2. Jazz musicians exploring modal improvisation have written some popular "modal blues" where the changes don't faithfully follow the three-chord format. For example, tunes such as *Footprints* by Wayne Shorter or Miles Davis' *All Blues*, which adds some spice to the turnaround by adding a substitution.

We're going to use the changes of *All Blues* to illustrate two approaches to soloing over dominant chord vamps. One will give us a classic bebop sound, and the other will create a more modern-sounding vocabulary.

(NB: You can also use the ideas here for strict one-chord vamp tunes such as *Freedom Jazz Dance* by Eddie Harris, or its modern contrafact, *Do Like Eddie* by John Scofield, based on a static Bb7).

The Minorization Approach

One of the keys to the improvised lines of jazz guitar giant Pat Martino is understanding that he viewed all chords as minor tonalities. His preference for using minor scales/arpeggios meant that when he was confronted with a dominant 7 chord, he would visualize a minor chord or scale superimposed on top of it. This superimposition would give him easy access to all the sounds he wanted to hear.

Martino's favored approach was to play minor arpeggios or scales a perfect 5th above the root of a dominant 7 chord. The table below shows the chord changes of *All Blues* and the arpeggios/scales Pat would think of when improvising – each a 5th above the root of the chord.

All Blues chords	G7	C7	D7#9	Eb7#9
Minorization	Dm7, Dm9, Dm6 arpeggios; the D Melodic Minor scale	Gm7, Gm9, Gm6 arpeggios; the G Melodic Minor scale	Am7, Am9, Am6 arpeggios; the A Melodic Minor scale	Bbm7, Bbm9, Bbm6 arpeggios; the Bb Melodic Minor scale

You can see that this is a modal approach to the blues, rather than thinking around a single key center.

Although the idea of thinking entirely in superimpositions is potentially mind-boggling, it's a concept most players quickly get into, because it's about repurposing things we already know. Plus, the interval of a 5th is very easy to locate and visualize on guitar.

We'll ease into this idea by initially playing some arpeggio-focused lines. Then we'll move onto scale superimposition ideas. Finally, we'll use both devices and also add some chromatic passing notes in the bebop tradition to target the strong chord tones. Let's go!

The chord progression for *All Blues* runs as follows and the tune is played in 6/8 time:

| G7 | % | % | % |

| C7 | % | G7 | % |

| D7#9 | Eb7#9 D7#9 | G7 | % |

As a simple illustration of the sound the superimposition concept creates, this first example is played over the static G7 section of the tune and uses only the notes of a basic Dm7 arpeggio (D, F, A, C).

It's important to understand how the notes of Dm7 function over the G7 harmony. The D and F notes are shared by both chords (D is the 5th, and F the b7 of G7). The A and C notes add some color. In relation to G7, A is the 9th and C is the 11th.

Here's how that sounds. It instantly creates a more sophisticated sound that takes us away from blues or pentatonic clichés.

Example 3a

The melodic possibilities instantly become richer when we extend this arpeggio to become a Dm9 (D, F, A, C, E). The E note this adds is the 13th of G7. It's a good idea to break up the rhythm of arpeggio-based licks to prevent them from sounding too predictable.

Example 3b

The other Martino option (also much used by Wes Montgomery), is the Dm6 arpeggio (D, F, A, B), from which we can create melodic ideas like the example below. The B note is the 3rd of the G7 chord, so a strong note to launch from.

For the fingering in bar one, I favor playing the 4th string 9th fret with the first finger, then quickly moving the hand into 10th position to play the 10th fret notes also with the first finger.

Example 3c

We've played three lines over the first four bars of this blues, but we also need to apply this idea to the other sections. Let's use what we've learned over the C7 – G7 chord change. Here, we'll use G minor arpeggios for the C7 chord and seek to move seamlessly into D minor arpeggio ideas for the G7 chord.

In bars 1-2, the melodic line is built from a Gm9 arpeggio, and in bars 3-4 from a Dm9 arpeggio. The latter begins on the last note of bar two, anticipating the chord change.

Example 3d

In the final four bars of the *All Blues* sequence, we need to dovetail together *three* sets of minor arpeggio superimpositions.

For the D7#9 chord we'll use A minor arpeggios, for Eb7#9 we'll use Bb minor arpeggios, then we're back to D minor for the G7 chord. Here's how we might construct a line around those changes.

Example 3e

You've probably already appreciated the fact that there is a lot of woodshedding to be done here. The lines we can create using arpeggio substitutions are infinitely more interesting than playing lots of pentatonic blues licks (though of course they have their important place). But… we need to know our arpeggio shapes thoroughly across the fretboard, then hone our ability to switch between them in different key centers.

In short, there's a lot of work to be done here in order to become fluent and get the most out of this idea, but if you want to dig deeper into the concept of soloing with arpeggios, my book *Jazz Book Arpeggio Soloing* provides a thorough workout.

My purpose in this book, however, is to give you lots of concepts to explore that will open up new sounds in your playing, so we're going to move on to the next stage: exploring the same set of superimposition ideas but this time using the melodic minor scale.

First, let's hear the sound of the D Melodic Minor scale superimposed over the G7 chord. D Melodic Minor contains the notes D, E, F, G, A, B, C#.

Example 3f

The melodic minor scale will add another layer of sophistication to your lines. Using your ears is really important here, as you become familiar with how the intervals interact with the chord. I think the best approach to apply this idea is to learn the scale thoroughly across the fretboard, then use your ears and personal taste to determine which notes sound most pleasing to you against the harmony.

Here's another example of superimposing D Melodic Minor over G7.

Example 3g

For the chord IV to chord I change, we'll use G Melodic Minor over C7, moving into D Melodic Minor over G7.

This example is played in 1/8th note triplets and needs some thought to match the note interval choices to the continuous triplet pattern. Over both chords a "doubling-back" sequence is played, but the pattern changes in bars 3-4 as the line ascends on one string.

Example 3h

Here's another example of this idea, playing with the rhythm.

Example 3i

Over the turnaround, we need to dovetail together A Melodic Minor (D7), Bb Melodic Minor (Eb7) and D Melodic Minor (G7) scales. When doing this, we're looking for the next closest note as we change scales, which of course demands we have a good working knowledge of each one.

Example 3j

Here's another example of the above approach, this time beginning with a motif idea, which helps to tie together the transition between scales.

Example 3k

To create some really authentic bebop vocabulary, we can begin combine arpeggios and scales, then add chromatic passing or approach notes.

Chromatic notes can add momentum to an ascending or descending run, and can also add a sense of "gravity" when we target chord tones on the strong beats of the bar.

Let's work through the *All Blues* progression again, and I'll point out where we're playing arpeggio shapes with approach notes and chromatically enhancing scale runs.

First, a D Melodic Minor based line with passing notes, built around a 5th position Dm7 arpeggio.

Example 3l

This scale-based line targets the b7 of the G7 chord on the first beat of bar one, and again at the beginning of bar two. The E note in bar three is the 13th of G7.

Example 3m

Chromatic notes are added into the descending and ascending runs here, over the chord IV to I change. A pedal tone lick in bar three adds some contrast.

Example 3n

This idea begins by visualizing a standard C7 barre chord in 8th position. At the end of bar two, a chromatic descent targets the B note of the D Melodic Minor scale on the first beat of bar three. Bars 3-4 are a D Melodic Minor scale-based idea.

Example 3o

We're back at the turnaround and moving from A Melodic Minor into Bb Melodic Minor into D Melodic Minor, looking for nearest note connections between the three scales. This time we're doing that with chromatic note targeting to create a more complex harmonic line.

Example 3p

Here's one final example of this approach, beginning with a cascading descending A Melodic Minor line with some chromatics. It transitions smoothly into Bb Melodic Minor via a half step movement. At the end of bar two, the D root of D Melodic Minor (and the 5th of G7) is played early to anticipate the chord change.

Example 3q

The Lydian Dominant (aka Mixolydian #4) Approach

For a more modern sound over a standard like *All Blues* the Lydian Dominant sound is definitely worth exploring. You'll hear it in the improvisation of players like Kurt Rosenwinkel, Jonathan Kreisberg, John Scofield and others.

The Lydian Dominant scale is played from the root note of a dominant 7 chord. E.g., over G7 we use the G Lydian Dominant scale, and over C7 we use the C Lydian Dominant scale, etc.

To keep things simple, all the examples here are played over a static G7 chord. Your mission over coming practice sessions is to learn and apply the relevant Lydian Dominant scales to the other chords in the *All Blues* progression.

So, where does this scale come from and why does it sound so cool?

The Lydian Dominant scale is virtually identical to the Mixolydian mode, apart from one note. Compare G Mixolydian to G Lydian Dominant in the table below.

G Mixolydian	G	A	B	C	D	E	F
G Lydian Dominant	G	A	B	C#	D	E	F

The Lydian Dominant's sharpened 4th interval is why it's also known as the Mixolydian #4 scale in Berklee circles.

G Lydian Dominant is the fourth mode of the parent scale of D Melodic Minor and acts as a kind of bridge between dominant and minor sounds.

At this point you might be thinking, "Hang on, Martino plays D Melodic Minor over G7, and essentially so do guys like Kurt Rosenwinkel… it's just another way of saying the same thing!"

Well, not quite.

Although we're working with a similar group of notes, in practice these two concepts are applied quite differently. You'll hear the distinction once you begin playing the examples below.

The classic bebop approach is to pepper arpeggio/scale patterns with chromatic approach notes that weave around target chord tones. The Rosenwinkel way of improvising with the Lydian Dominant is more intervallic, uses more pure scale tones, and handles chromatics differently.

The approach taken by Kurt and others (Mike Stern for example), is to break down the scale into its diatonic triads and arpeggios and think in terms of cellular melodic ideas that are woven alongside long, flowing scalic passages. Mike Stern in particular breaks up scales by playing intervallic patterns, such as diatonic 4ths.

Let's begin by looking at some intervallic ideas over the G7 bars of *All Blues*, using the G Lydian Dominant scale.

This first idea is an ascending run in "fours". In other words, ascending the G Lydian Dominant scale four notes from its root, then doubling back to ascend four notes from the second note of the scale (A) etc. To make things more complicated, we're playing the "fours" in 1/16th note triplets. We break away from the fours pattern and the triplets midway through bar two.

Example 3r

In bars 1-2 of this line we are descending G Lydian Dominant in "fives" using the same principle as the previous example. Because the groups of five don't fit neatly into a measure, the result is a melodic idea that flows over the bar line.

From the last note of bar two onwards, we begin a new melodic idea. Here, the idea is to play five-note "cells" and although the line begins with two lots of ascending fives, we don't stick to that pattern.

Example 3s

This time we begin by ascending in diatonic 4th intervals from the G root. From beat 3 of bar two, we break out of this pattern to play six-note cells in a descending motif.

Example 3t

Here's one final intervallic idea. This one uses ascending diatonic 5ths in bars 1-2. You can break up a pattern like this any way you like by punctuating it with rests or altering the lengths of certain notes.

From the latter half of bar three, we are creating four-note cells that ascend the scale stepwise on the second string. The cellular pattern could be any group of four notes that sit close together on the fretboard, as long as the leading note is moving stepwise through the scale to tie the line together.

Example 3u

Next, we'll look at some melodic lines that use triad pairs from the Lydian Dominant. We looked at this idea briefly in Chapter Two with the melodic minor scale. If we harmonize the G Lydian Dominant scale by stacking notes in 3rds, we get the set of triads shown in the table below. The table also shows the 7th chords that are created if we extend these triads.

G	A	B	C#	D	E	F
G major	A major	B dim.	C# dim.	D minor	E minor	F aug.
G7	A7	Bm7b5	C#m7b5	Dmin(Maj7)	Em7	FMaj7#5

We'll start with a really easy example that uses the G and A major triads. It's an obvious idea to play – one that you might even use as a practice drill – but it serves to highlight the effect of combining the triads over the G7 harmony.

The notes of the G major triad (G, B, D) all belong to the G7 chord, of course. But the A, C# and E notes of the A major triad create, respectively, 9th, #11 and 13th intervals over G7. The triad combination gives us a nice mix of inside notes, extended notes, and one altered note.

Example 3v

Things get more interesting when we begin to understand the bigger pattern of the two triads across the fretboard and freely mix them up – both via our note choices and rhythms.

This line came together by considering how the triad notes combined around 3rd position on the neck, then moving up into 7th position.

Example 3w

Here is another line initially built around 3rd position. Here we play a G major triad, followed by a partial A major triad. We've left the 3rd out of the latter, but it creates a nice melodic line over two octaves.

Example 3x

I'm an advocate of using triad pairs in a less obvious way, focused around a position on the fretboard and applying the six notes as a type of hybrid scale. I recommend practicing in this way with the assistance of a fretboard mapping tool to really understand the fretboard layout of the notes.

This line begins in 9th position. Visualize a 10th fret G13 chord with the root on the fifth string as a point of reference. At the end of bar one we play a five-note motif, and this is echoed in bar two, moving down the neck.

Example 3y

Let's try another triad pair from the harmonized Lydian Dominant scale. This time, D minor (D, F, A) and E minor (E, G, B). Here is a motif-driven line that ascends on the top two strings.

Example 3z

This example treats the triads like a hybrid scale and moves freely between them.

Example 3z1

This line take a more obvious triad pair approach to construct the melody. The lick starts with D minor triad inversions moving into E minor triad inversions, followed by a sparse melodic phrase in bar two. In bar three, the first descending motif combines notes from both triads and is followed up with a D minor triad. An E minor triad spans the end of bar three into bar four, and we end back where we started with a D minor triad inversion.

Example 3z2

Let's switch triad pairs again and work with the two diminished triads that occur within the scale: Bdim (B, D, F) and C#dim (C#, E, G).

By now you'll probably have noticed that all of these triad pairs have many notes in common, so why not just work with the scale since it contains all of the notes? There are two good reasons:

1. We work with triads because they are very strong melodic structures, and combining them enables us to play more interesting intervallic ideas that contain wider leaps.

2. When we select and work with a new triad pair, even if just one note changes, the entire fretboard pattern alters, and new shapes emerge from which we can build melodic ideas. There is no doubt that we'll be inspired to play different ideas using two diminished triads than we did when using two minor or major triads.

Let's hear how the diminished triads sound.

Example 3z3 starts by ascending Bdim and C#dim triads. In bar two, the ringing three-note phrase combines notes from both triads, then moves into a descending motif that uses two notes from each triad (with one combined exception).

Example 3z3

Try this 1/16th note triplet idea that begins with Bdim and C#dim ascending triads, then moves into a pedal tone idea, with notes on the top two strings bouncing off a constant C# to D movement on the third string.

Example 3z4

Now for a line that treats the two triads like a hybrid scale. The intervals of the two diminished triads combined make for some beautifully exotic, modern sounding lines.

Example 3z5

Here's another idea using the same principle.

Example 3z6

To wrap up this section, here's a diminished triad pair line that begins with a Kurt Rosenwinkel-style legato run. Kurt would downpick the first of each group of notes and play the rest using hammer-ons.

Example 3z7

(NB: It's important to note here that we can also combine triads of different qualities e.g., major and minor or diminished and augmented. This is something we'll explore in Chapter Five).

To close out this chapter, however, I want us to consider one final idea for our modal melodic explorations.

Cellular Thinking

Let's remind ourselves of the notes of the G Lydian Dominant scale:

G, A, B, C#, D, E, F

We can select four notes from this collection of intervals and work with them to create four-note cellular permutations – similar to the approach taken by John Coltrane and Michael Brecker.

Considering that we're playing over a G7 chord, we could for example opt to use the notes B, F, A and C#. Over G7 that gives us the chord's guide tones (B and F, the 3rd and b7), plus the 9th (A) and the #11 (C#). In other words, we can select notes on the basis of how "inside" or "outside" we want our cellular ideas to sound.

Or we can opt to use one of the four-note 7th chords that occur naturally in the scale. You'll recall that there is one augmented triad contained in the scale. If we extend this to a 7th chord, F augmented becomes FMaj7#5. This chord has the notes F (b7), A (9th), C# (#11) and E (13th). This will create a more outside sound, because we don't have the root or 3rd of the chord in the cell.

Let's take the FMaj7#5 arpeggio and see what melodic ideas it yields. The idea is to stick to the four-note cellular structure in our phrasing, but we can play the notes in any order we choose, and also repeat notes to complete a cell. Play this first example and you'll get the idea.

The first and most obvious idea to emerge from this arpeggio is to play four-note cells using just the augmented triad and one repeated note. Augmented triads move across the fretboard in major 3rd intervals, as in bar two here where we're playing 1/16th notes with a four-against-three feel.

Rhythmically, this is a tricky line to play as we move from four-against-three 1/16th notes to straight 1/16th notes into triplet 1/16th notes in four-note groupings. Listen to the audio a few times and practice it slowly until you have all the rhythms in place.

Example 3z8

Next, a Brecker-type line played mostly in 1/16th notes. We're sticking rigidly to the four-note cell approach, but the line is broken up rhythmically with occasional 1/16th note rests and a single 1/8th note in bar three.

Example 3z9

The previous two examples sounded full of tension because we kept our distance from the guide tones of the underlying G7. But we can select any four notes from the parent scale and combine intervals that sound less challenging. For example, G (root), B (3rd), A (9th) and E (13th). This line begins and ends on a chord tone.

Example 3z10

Or how about the previously suggested B, F, A and C#, respectively the 3rd, b7, 9th and #11 – a nice mix of the guide tones plus one extended and one altered note.

Although we're now much closer to the G7 harmony, the line still sounds like contemporary jazz vocabulary due to the inclusion of the #11 tone, plus the fact that we're playing wide intervals, avoiding the stepwise predictability of a scalic approach.

Example 3z11

There's a great deal to explore in this idea and space won't allow us to go much deeper, but I encourage you to dig into this concept in your practice times. Experiment with four-note cells using different note combinations from the Lydian Dominant scale and audition the sounds you create. Over time you'll uncover the ideas that really represent your unique sound and style.

Chapter Four – Major 7 & Major 7#11 Vamps

In this chapter we'll explore soloing options for tunes that have multiple bars of static major 7 or major 7#11 chords. Before getting into the examples, I recommend listening to these classic standards, most of which use both types of chord:

- *Little Sunflower* – Freddie Hubbard

- *Forest Flower* – Charles Lloyd

- *Deluge* – Wayne Shorter

- *Havona* – Jaco Pastorius

Major 7 Chords

Little Sunflower by Freddie Hubbard is an uber-cool modal tune built around a D Dorian vamp, but with an 8-bar bridge section consisting of four bars of EbMaj7 and four bars of DMaj7. The bridge is played twice before returning to the Dm7 vamp. We'll use this tune as our workhorse throughout this chapter and explore some ideas over those major 7 chords.

(As an aside, it's worth checking out the album *Backlash* from which this tune comes – renowned as one of Hubbard's greatest recordings).

What strategies can we use to elevate our soloing vocabulary over the ubiquitous major 7 chord? I'm going to recommend two approaches that will modernize your melodic lines, at the same time opening up the fretboard to help you avoid falling into the same old patterns and licks.

1. Relative Minor Pentatonic Approach x 3

In Chapter One we looked at the "three-pronged" minor pentatonic approach. We can use that idea again, the difference being that we'll be play minor pentatonic scales from the *relative minor* of the major 7 chord.

The first major 7 chord we encounter in *Little Sunflower* is EbMaj7. The relative minor key of Eb Major is C Minor, so the first pentatonic scale we'll use is C Minor Pentatonic.

Then, just as we did in Chapter One, we'll move up a whole step to play D Minor Pentatonic, then play the scale a perfect 5th above the first scale i.e., moving into G Minor Pentatonic.

Over the EbMaj7 chord our note choices will come from these three minor pentatonic scales, which we'll apply individually as well as moving freely between them. Each five-note scale has a different effect when played over the major 7 chord. In relation to EbMaj7:

- **C Minor Pentatonic** gives us the 13th, root, 9th, 3rd and 5th (C, Eb, F, G, Bb) and is the most inside sound

- **D Minor Pentatonic** gives us the 7th, 9th, 3rd, #11 and 13th (D, F, G, A, C) and has a nice balance of guide tones, extended notes, and one altered note

- **G Minor Pentatonic** gives us the 3rd, 5th, 13th, 7th and 9th (G, Bb, C, D, F). Its effect is similar to C Minor Pentatonic but it does not contain the Eb root note of the chord, replacing it with a D, so has a more open, ambiguous sound

One of the great benefits of thinking in terms of three pentatonic scales as options for improvisation is that it immediately opens up the fretboard and takes us away from just thinking "Eb Major scale". That helps us to break away from the clichéd ideas we might normally go for.

Let's look at a collection of examples that use this idea. First, an example using only the G Minor Pentatonic scale. The line weaves between EbMaj7 guide tones and extended notes but avoids the root. The result is a nice spacious sound.

Example 4a

Now let's try C Minor Pentatonic, which contains the Eb root note. Starting in the middle of the neck, this line works its way into the higher register to play a sequenced pattern that highlights the root and 9th of the underlying EbMaj7 chord on the top string.

Example 4b

Next, let's audition the D Minor Pentatonic scale, which contains the #11 interval when played over EbMaj7, and omits the root note. This line leans on the fact that many notes in the scale sit in 4th intervals on the fretboard.

Example 4c

Next, let's combine the G Minor and D Minor Pentatonic scales. This is one of my favorite things to do and can result in some lush lines over EbMaj7.

Example 4d

Here's another example that weaves between G Minor and D Minor Pentatonic. This line makes a feature of the A note belonging to D Minor Pentatonic to imply an EbMaj7#11 harmony.

Example 4e

If we combine the C and D Minor Pentatonic scales and switch between them, we can create motifs that move in whole steps. Taking this approach also means we can easily move between inside (C Minor Pentatonic) and more outside (D Minor Pentatonic) sounds.

Example 4f

Here's a short sequenced line in 1/16th notes. Bar one is C Minor Pentatonic and bar two is D Minor Pentatonic. Again, we've just moved the motif up a whole step, but because the line moves continuously, and the two scales share notes in common, the shift is less obvious than in the previous example.

Example 4g

There is a lot of mileage to be had from the sequencing approach. In this sequence, we are still shifting from C to D Minor Pentatonic, allocating a bar to each, but we're not simply moving the pattern up a whole step. Instead, we repeat the rhythmic phrasing, but access a different pentatonic shape for the D Minor Pentatonic line.

Example 4h

The next two examples combine all three pentatonic scales, moving from G Minor to D Minor to C Minor Pentatonic. To make the scale transitions less obvious, we're changing midway through some of the bars.

Example 4i

To finish this section, here's a long 1/16th note line in the style of Michael Brecker – a master at moving through series of superimposed scales over static chord vamps. Where you see notes repeated on the top string, this signifies a fretting hand position change.

Example 4j

There is a lot of scope for developing this pentatonic language, so make sure to spend some time jamming with the scales over the backing track and see what ideas you can come up with.

Remember too that you can transpose all of these ideas down a half step to play them over the DMaj7 section of *Little Sunflower* (in which case you'd be using the B Minor, C# Minor and F# Minor Pentatonic scales).

2. The Lydian scale

The three-pronged pentatonic approach is useful because it allows us the option of picking just one pentatonic scale to play lines with wider intervals, or combining scales to create more sophisticated lines – all using the robust pentatonic patterns we know so well.

A great alternative to this approach is to play the Lydian mode from the root of the major 7 chord.

We'll turn our focus now to the DMaj7 bars of the *Little Sunflower*, which transition back into the Dm7 vamp. Over DMaj7 we'll play the D Lydian scale, and when we move to Dm7 we'll use D Dorian.

D Lydian comprises the notes D, E, F#, G#, A, B, C#

It's almost identical to the D Major scale, but contains a #4 interval (G# instead of G) which makes a world of difference to the sound it creates. When played over a DMaj7 chord, it implies the richer harmony of DMaj7#11.

D Lydian is the fourth mode of the A Major parent scale, so when we play D Lydian over DMaj7, it's like playing in A Major. However, it's much better to learn the Lydian scale from its root note and treat it as a unique sound in its own right.

Before you jump into the melodic examples, play through these D Lydian scale CAGED patterns across the neck. In the examples that follow, we'll think in terms of these shapes/positions and move between them. D root notes are indicated with a square.

D Lydian "C" Shape   D Lydian "A" Shape   D Lydian "G" Shape

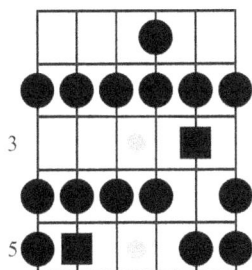

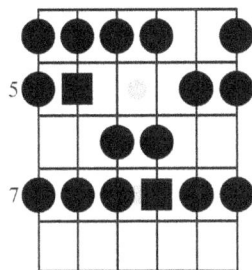

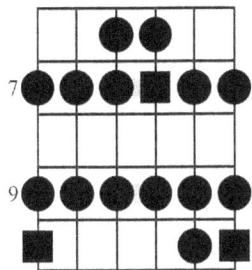

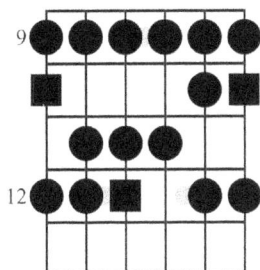

D Lydian "E" Shape   D Lydian "D" Shape

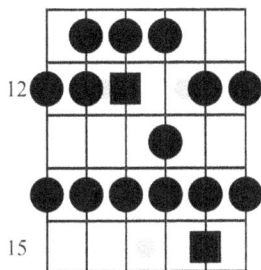

This line starts in the D Lydian "C" Shape, which we use for bars 1-2. In bar three we shift position into the adjacent "A" Shape. We then briefly transition back into the "C" midway through bar four, before moving up into 5th position to play a Dorian lick over Dm7.

Example 4k

This melodic idea uses the "E" Shape for the entire line. To move into the Dm7 section, we target an E note on the first string, 12th fret – a note common to both scales. The Dorian lick contains one non-scale note – a chromatic approach note from below, midway through bar five.

Example 4l

Next, a line that begins in the D Lydian "E" Shape and ascends into the "D" Shape using 1/8th note triplets. At the end of bar four, a B "pivot" note shared by D Lydian and D Dorian is used to transition to the Dm7 chord. In bar five we use a Dm6 arpeggio.

Example 4m

This idea moves between shapes "A" and "G" using a six-note motif that repeats throughout. To move from the "G" shape into a 5th position D Dorian shape, we can do so on the third string with an idea that sounds like a chromatic run but is really just hopping from one shape to the next.

Example 4n

In bar one of this example we are playing just the initial notes of each scale shape in a four-note motif, ascending through the CAGED shapes in order. In order to learn where the shapes lie on the fretboard, moving through them on one string is a great way to train your ears with the intervals.

From bar two onwards we're working with the D Lydian "E" shape, and in bar four use it to transition smoothly into a D Dorian line based around 10th position. I added a chromatic run into the end of the Dorian lick.

Example 4o

This line moves between the "C" and "A" shapes of D Lydian. To get the most out of the scale patterns and avoid just running up and down them, aim to create melodic, motif-led ideas, and include techniques such as pedal tones or rhythmic diversity to keep the interest going.

Example 4p

An Alternative Option for the Major7#11 Chord

If you're playing a modal jazz tune where the harmony specifically states a major 7#11 chord is to be played, then the Lydian scale is an obvious choice because it contains the chord's #11 (the major 7#11 is often referred to simply as "the Lydian chord").

However, if you want to create a really modern, edgy sound over this chord, you can also play the melodic minor scale played from the relative minor of the major 7#11.

The tunes *Deluge* by Wayne Shorter and *Havona* by Jaco Pastorius contain several measures of an EMaj7#11 chord.

Over EMaj7#11 we can play either:

- The E Lydian scale (mode 4 of the parent key B Major)

- The C# Melodic Minor scale

66

The relative minor key to E Major is C# Minor. This is just a simple way of remembering that over EMaj7#11 we can creates melodies using the C# Melodic Minor scale.

So, why does this idea work?

EMaj7#11 contains the notes E, G#, B, D#, A#

The C# Melodic Minor scale has the notes: C#, D#, E, F#, G#, A#, B#

This scale contains four chord tones of EbMaj7#11 then adds the 9th and 13th. It's similar to the E Lydian scale but the melodic minor has a #5 interval, compared to the Lydian's natural 5th. This note makes a significant difference to the tension the scale creates. Let's explore this sound with a few example lines.

To get started, play this line launching from 4th position and listen to how the scale works over the major 7#11 chord.

Example 4q

This scalic idea includes a straight ascent of the C# Melodic Minor scale in bar two. In bar three a passing C note is added to give the line a little bebop flavor.

Example 4r

Whatever scale you happen to be working with, a melodic approach can always be found by breaking it down into its diatonic triads. Triads have a strong, stable sound and lend themselves to creating dynamic sequences. The example below spells out which triads from C# Melodic Minor are being used in the line.

Example 4s

We can create spacious sounding lines with wider intervals by choosing just one diatonic arpeggio to work with – in this case the B#m7b5 arpeggio from C# Melodic Minor, superimposed over EMaj7#11.

Example 4t

Let's repeat that idea, this time using only the A#m7b5 arpeggio from the scale, developed into an ascending motif.

Example 4u

The next example returns to a scale sequence idea. Here we mix up the rhythmic phrasing to keep things interesting.

Example 4v

The final couple of examples show how we might solo over the whole A Section of *Deluge*, which has six bars of EbMaj7#11 followed by a bar of Ebm7 and a bar of A7#11.

First, a motif-led idea from C# Melodic Minor, leading into the melodic minor scale played from the root of the Ebm7 chord, then the melodic minor a half step above the root of the A7 altered dominant chord (Bb Melodic Minor).

Example 4w

In this final example, after opening with a long rhythmic motif that continues through bars 1-4, in bar five we switch to short, mainly four-note phrasing to set up another rhythmic motif. In bars 6-7 we are drawing on diatonic triads from C# Melodic Minor: C#m transitioning into Ebm, indicated above the notation.

For the A7#11 chord in bar eight, we're thinking Bb Melodic Minor again and using the Db augmented triad from that scale to create an altered sound.

Example 4x

Chapter Five – 7sus4 Chord Vamps

No exploration of modal jazz tunes would be complete without addressing the dominant 7sus4 chord. In this chapter we'll look at the classic standard *Maiden Voyage* by Herbie Hancock, which uses 7sus4 chords with shifting tonal centers throughout, and explore how we can solo over it with well-conceived melodic phrases.

First, a word about how the 7sus4 chord is constructed.

Dominant 7 chords are formed by stacking the root, 3rd, 5th and b7 degrees of the major scale. E.g.:

D7 = D (root), F# (3rd), A (5th), C (b7)

In the 7sus4 chord, the 3rd is replaced with the 4th interval of the parent scale:

D7sus4 = D (root), G (4th), A (5th), C (b7)

The 4th interval creates the "suspension" that strongly wants to resolve down to the 3rd. However, in most modal compositions the 7sus4 chord doesn't resolve, and we're left with this ambiguous sounding chord.

NB: Note that on some lead sheets, you'll see the D7sus4 chord written as "D9sus". This is just a D7sus4 voicing that also includes the 9th i.e., D, E, G, A, C.

Seeing the 7sus4 chord on a lead sheet has baffled many a guitar player. What scale fits over this chord? Do we have to avoid the 3rd, since the chord replaces it with the 4th?

Let's dive in and discover some different sounds that work over this chord. We'll use the A section of *Maiden Voyage* to test our ideas. The chord changes are:

| D7sus4 | % | % | % |

| F7sus4 | % | % | % |

Something that immediately stands out about this progression is the minor 3rd shift from D to F. This opens up the possibility of transposing any melodic idea we think of up a minor 3rd – a commonly heard technique in modern jazz, and an idea we'll use in some of the examples ahead.

Before we get to that, let's test out a number of ideas over just the first four bars – a D7sus4 vamp.

Approach 1: Superimposing minor ideas a perfect 5th above

The "minor a 5th above" substitution works nicely in this context. We can simplify our approach to the D7sus4 chord and just think "A minor".

First, we can work with arpeggios, and an Am9 arpeggio works beautifully over this chord. It contains the notes A, C, E, G, B, and when superimposed over D7sus4, those intervals represent the 5th, b7, 9th, 4th and 13th of the dominant chord. Listen to how it sounds.

Example 5a

Here's another line based around an Am9 arpeggio. I think it creates a bright, optimistic sound over the ambiguous 7sus4.

Example 5b

This Am9 arpeggio driven line begins with a descending 1/8th note triplet run. In bar two the line transitions into a fast, two-note-per-string ascending run. This is a nice line to memorize because it spells out a useful pattern for playing any arpeggio with only small adjustments needed.

Example 5c

If we omit the A note of an Am9 chord we're left with four notes that also spell Cmaj7. In bar one here, you'll recognize the common Cmaj7 shape that descends from the top string 7th fret.

Example 5d

Still thinking in terms of an A minor tonal center, we can turn to scales rather than arpeggios to create some interesting ideas, and the A Dorian scale works nicely over D7sus4.

A Dorian has the notes A, B, C, D, E, F#, and G. You may spot that it contains an F# note – the 3rd of a plain D7 chord, which gets replaced by a G note in D7sus4. However, the F# is *not* an avoid note. We can use it like an approach note, targeting the 4th (G) from a half step below.

Example 5e

This example ascends the A Dorian scale in 5th intervals in bar one, then plays a sequence arranged in 3rds in bar two, before moving into a rhythmic motif with a call and response phrasing.

Example 5f

Next, a fast descending A Dorian run followed by a slower ascending pattern. In bar one, we play an eight-note phrase, then jump back to begin another eight-note phrase. There are lots of different note groupings you could apply to the scale to invent new ideas, and this is just one idea – it's definitely worth experimenting to find your own.

Example 5g

Here's another line that presents a little challenge in terms of picking speed, accuracy and timing. It's nearly all 1/32nd notes, but the phrasing is broken up with rests. Years ago, I learned a great tip from my mentor, the great jazz guitarist Adrian Ingram. He told me that it wasn't necessary to play a constant stream of notes in order for a melodic line to sound "fast" – we can achieve the same effect using short bursts of notes. This is great advice, because it's hard to maintain a fast line over multiple bars without it sounding robotic and unmusical.

Notice here too where the rests are placed. We want the melodic lines to flow across the bar lines, not be constrained by them.

Example 5h

Approach 2: Phrygian Dominant Scale

For a more exotic, modern sound, we can use the D Phrygian Dominant scale (D, Eb, F#, G, A, Bb, C) to form ideas over D7sus4. Over this chord, the scale notes, in order, represent the root, b9, 3rd, 4th, 5th, #5/b13 and b7.

The Phrygian Dominant is the fifth mode of the Harmonic Minor scale, so if you prefer to think in terms of a scale you already know rather than learning a new one, you can also think of this idea as playing the Harmonic Minor scale a perfect 5th *below* the root of the 7sus4 chord i.e., G Harmonic Minor over D7sus4. Here's how it sounds:

Example 5i

Here's a scale sequencing idea using D Phrygian Dominant. The two-note motif here is simply to play scale notes a half step apart, beginning with a higher note, then descending a half step.

Example 5j

This brisk 1/16th note line captures the exotic sound of the Phrygian Dominant and emphasizes the scale's half step intervals by going back and forth between them. The line ends with some deliberate tension by dropping an F# note on a downbeat. This is the 3rd of D7, but the D7sus4 has replaced that note with a G, so it creates (a not unpleasant) dissonance.

Example 5k

Beginning on the root note of the chord on beat 1 of bar one helps to ground this line as it goes on to weave around D Phrygian Dominant scale tones.

Example 5l

This line begins simply, using scale tones moving in 5ths. Bar three begins on the b9 of the chord to give some tension to the line, and in bar four we drop another F# on a downbeat, partway through the bar.

Example 5m

Approach 3: Mixolydian Bebop scale

To take a more bebop direction in our sound, the Mixolydian Bebop scale is a great choice that will allow us to include chromatic phrasing in our lines. In the next group of examples we'll also increase the complexity by building lines over eight bars rather than four, moving from D7sus4 into F7sus4. As a result, we'll need to work with two scales:

Over D7sus4, we'll use the D Mixolydian Bebop scale (D, E, F#, G, A, B, C, C#)

Over F7sus4, we'll use the F Mixolydian Bebop scale (F, G, A, Bb, C, D, Eb, E)

The chromatic notes help us to add momentum to descending or ascending lines, as you'll hear in this first example.

Example 5n

When switching between scales, remember to look for a smooth point of transition where, ideally, we can change from one to the next with a half step movement.

Example 5o

We've explored the Mixolydian Bebop with some long flowing lines, so here's a sequence you can use, best played as hammer-ons. If you're used to learning scales in box shapes, it's well worth working on them ascending the neck on just a couple of strings, as this will help you make quick position changes and use more of the range of your instrument.

Example 5p

The next example begins with a motif, then morphs into a long passage of 1/8th note triplets.

Example 5q

The art of turning scales into melodies is a lifelong pursuit for every jazz musician. We don't want to just run up and down scales, we want to create meaningful melodies and allow scale runs to be a bridge between our melodic ideas. In this example, a recurring theme is a six-note motif that gets moved around the fretboard. Connecting ideas here include a straight 1/16th note ascending run, and a cascading descending 1/8th note triplet run to end.

Example 5r

Approach 4: Triad pairs

The final approach we'll look at over this tune is triad pairs. To make our melodic lines more cellular and Brecker-esque, we can extract triad pairs from any of the aforementioned scales in this chapter. The following examples are drawn from the Dorian and Phrygian Dominant modes.

From the A Dorian scale, useful triad pairs are: Am and Bm, Cmaj and Dmaj, and F#dim and Gmaj.

From the D Phrygian Dominant scale we can use Dmaj and Ebmaj, F#dim and Adim, and Gm and Cm.

We also need to modulate these ideas to an F tonal center when the chord changes, so there is quite a lot to think about here! Let's start simple by using all minor triads.

In this example, for the D7sus4 chord, from the A Dorian scale we are extracting the Am and Bm triads. For the F7sus4 chord we're using the C Dorian scale (a substitution idea we've used throughout the book – the minor scale a 5th above the root of the dominant chord) and extracting its Cm and Dm triads.

With these tools we can create cellular ideas with a more intervallic feel.

Example 5s

Here's an example that uses individual triads from A Dorian and C Dorian, but also mixes the notes freely, treating the triad pairs as hybrid six-note scales for a truly modern sound.

Example 5t

This example also uses the Dorian scale as our source of notes, but this time we extract the Cmaj and Dmaj triad pair from A Dorian to play over D7sus4, and the Bbmaj and Cm triad pair from C Dorian to play over F7sus4.

Example 5u

In this example, from A Dorian we put together the F#dim and Em triad pair, and from C Dorian, Adim and Bb major triads.

Example 5v

There is so much more we could explore here! I urge you to explore as many triad combinations as you can. But now we'll move onto the Phrygian Dominant mode.

For the D7sus4 chord, we can extract from the D Phrygian Dominant scale Gm and Cmaj triad pairs, the result of which is to add the 9th and b13 notes to the harmony.

For the F7sus4 chord, we can extract from the F Phrygian Dominant scale the Bbm and Cm triads, which achieves the same effect over the F chord.

Example 5w

Over the D7sus4 chord, combining F#dim and Gm triads creates some really nice tensions. For the F7sus4, we can shift the same pairing up a minor 3rd to Adim to Bbm. This example uses strictly alternating triad pairs throughout.

Example 5x

To play over the D7sus4 chord in this example, combining the F#dim and Bbaug triads that exist within D Phrygian Dominant is an interesting idea. The triads share one note in common: F#dim (**F#**, A, C), Bbaug (Bb, D, **F#**), so putting them together creates a hybrid pentatonic scale. Move everything up a minor 3rd for the F chord.

Example 5y

Here's one final example that uses this hybrid pentatonic idea.

Example 5z

Chapter 6 – Two Example Solos

To complete our journey into modal soloing ideas, here are two complete solos for you to work through. First, over the changes to *Little Sunflower*, then *Maiden Voyage*.

In this book we've explored lots of ideas. This was intentional, because I wanted to give you lots of options for building interesting, modern-sounding solos. Some of these concepts represent months of work in order to do them justice and absorb them into your musical vocabulary, as I'm sure you're already aware.

However, I'll recall two things that the great jazz guitarist Martin Taylor said to me before we dive into these solos. First, he once commented that he would often hear students "playing theory". Second, on a humorous note, he quipped, "No one goes home from a gig whistling the Phrygian Dominant mode, Tim!"

In other words, we mustn't fall into the trap of using techniques for their own sake and forget about playing melody. To that end, I've endeavored to keep these solos melodic, while still using a selection of the harmonic devices we've covered.

First, have a listen to the audio of the complete solo over *Little Sunflower*, to get a feel for where it's going, then work through the notation in sections.

Here is a breakdown of the ideas used in the solo.

1. The 3 x minor pentatonic scale approach is used frequently over the Dm7 chord:

   • D Minor Pentatonic (minor pentatonic from the root)

   • E Minor Pentatonic (minor pentatonic a whole step above the root)

   • A Minor Pentatonic (minor pentatonic a perfect fifth above the root)

2. The D Dorian scale over Dm7. (See bar seventeen for a D Dorian run that includes a couple of chromatic approach notes to fill out the line. See also bars 37-41 which feature an ascending D Dorian sequence).

3. For the EbMaj7 and Dmaj7 chords, the relative minor and relative minor pentatonic scales are used:

   • Over EbMaj7, C Natural Minor or C Minor Pentatonic

   • Over Dmaj7, B Natural Minor or B Minor Pentatonic

See bars 21-36, for example.

4. Triad pairs from the melodic minor scale. Particularly during the final sixteen bars of the solo, over the Dm7 chord, the melodic lines are built from a D minor and E minor triad pair. As I played, I was thinking D Melodic Minor, but these could also be seen as coming from D Dorian. Either way, rather than playing obvious, whole step movements to spell out the triad pairs, I treated them as a hybrid scale – a pool of six notes to choose from.

Example 6a

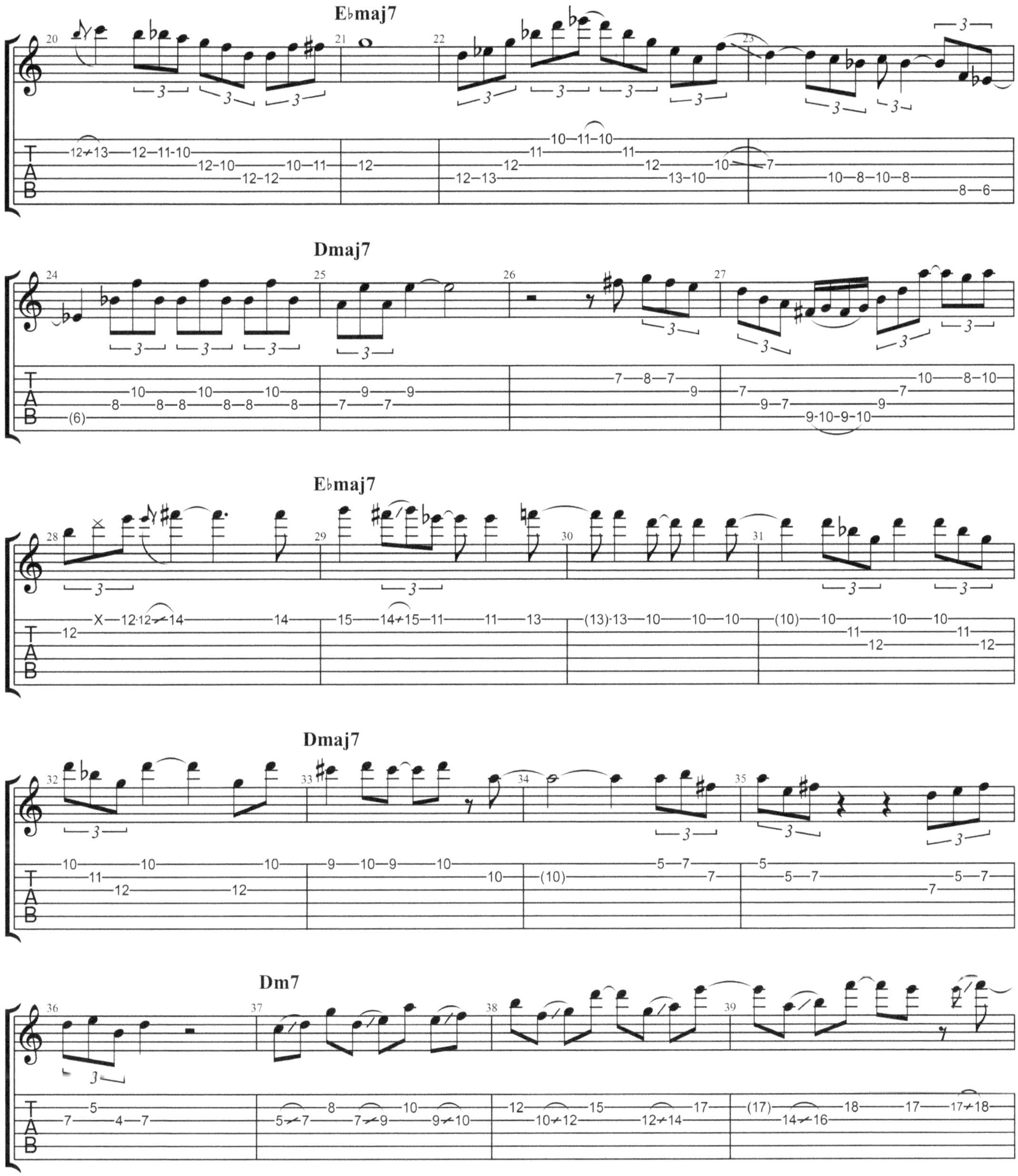
E♭maj7
Dmaj7
E♭maj7
Dmaj7
Dm7

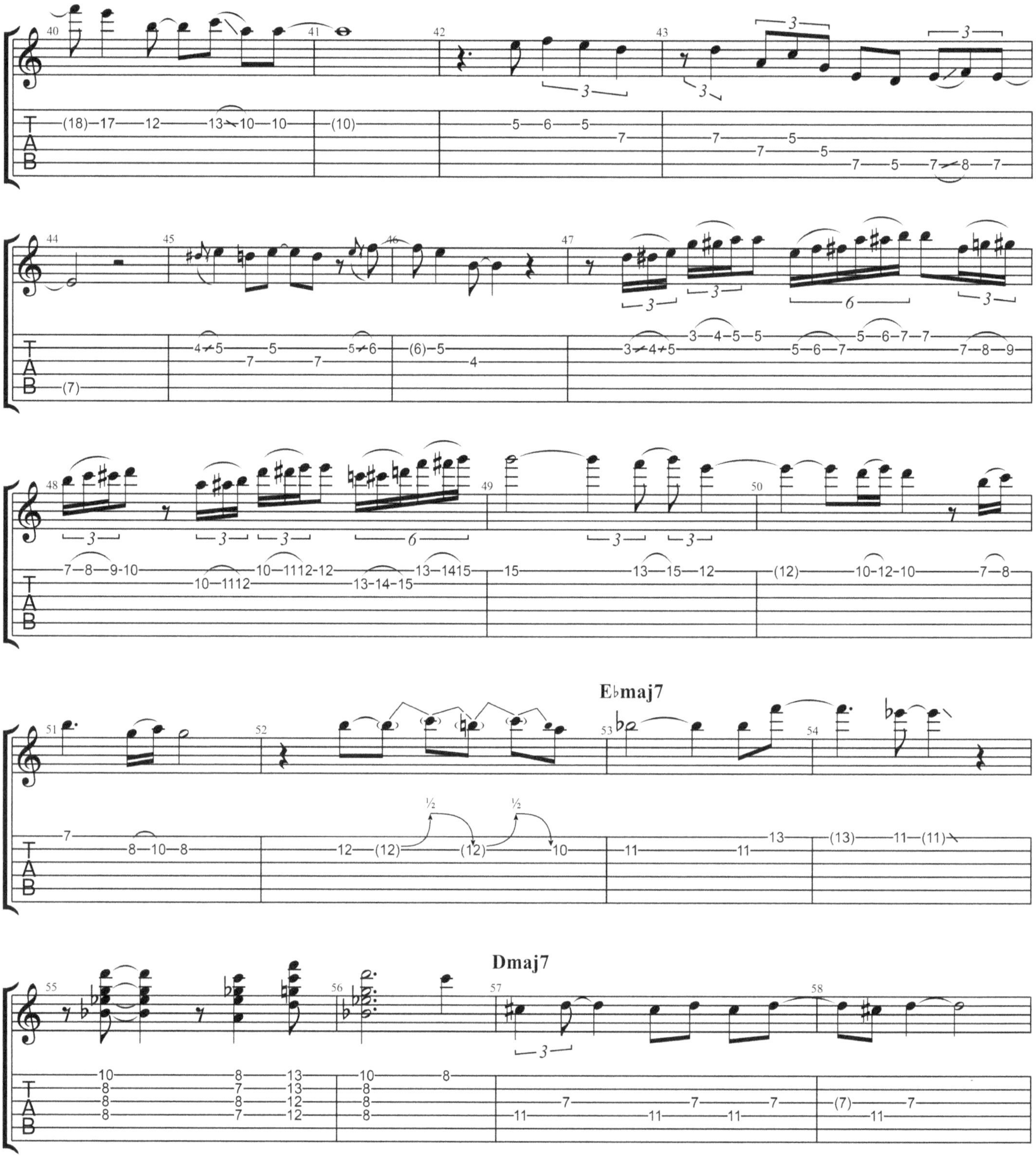
E♭maj7
Dmaj7

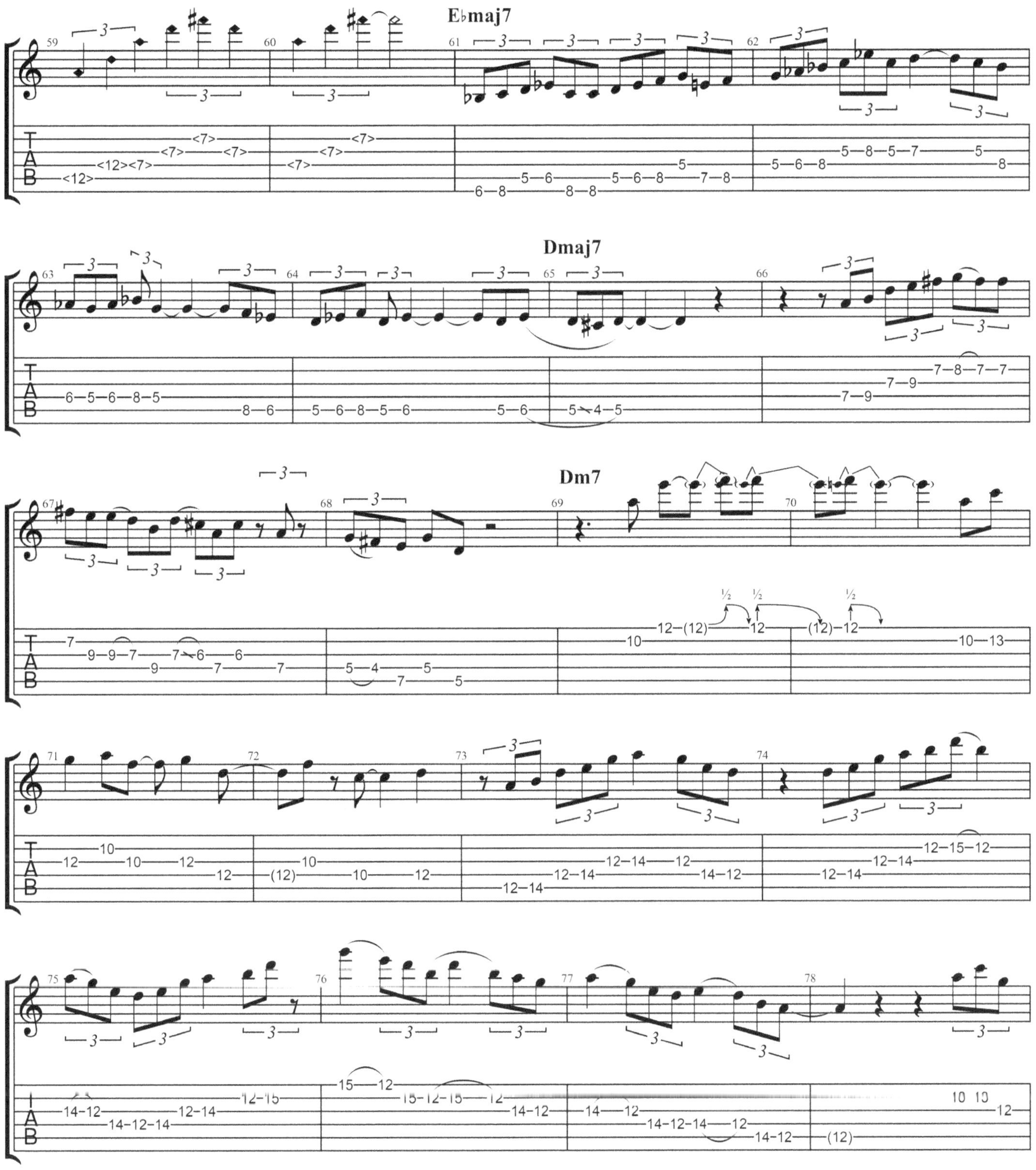
E♭maj7
Dmaj7
Dm7

Next, let's take a look at the second solo over the chord changes to *Maiden Voyage*. Here's a summary of the approaches used in the solo:

1. Minorization of dominant 9sus chords. As discussed in Chapter Four, we can simplify our thinking over the complex sounding D9sus and F9sus chords by minorizing them like Pat Martino:

- Over D9sus: A Dorian scale, Am9/CMaj7 arpeggios, or simply A Minor Pentatonic

- Over F9sus: C Dorian, Cm9/EbMaj7 arpeggios, C Minor Pentatonic

2. For a more exotic sound, we can apply the melodic minor scale in a minorization approach. You can see this in action in bars 17-20 of the solo, where the Bb Melodic Minor scale is played over Eb9sus. I.e., the melodic minor scale a perfect 5th above the root of the chord.

3. The *Maiden Voyage* changes have a four-bar section of C#m9. Here, an obvious choice is the C# Melodic Minor scale.

4. Triad pairs from the Phrygian Dominant scale are a great choice over the 9sus chords. Due to the open-sounding nature of the 9sus, this is one context in which it's helpful to spell out obvious triad pairs, rather than using a hybrid scale approach (as demonstrated in bar thirty-three over D9sus).

Example 6b

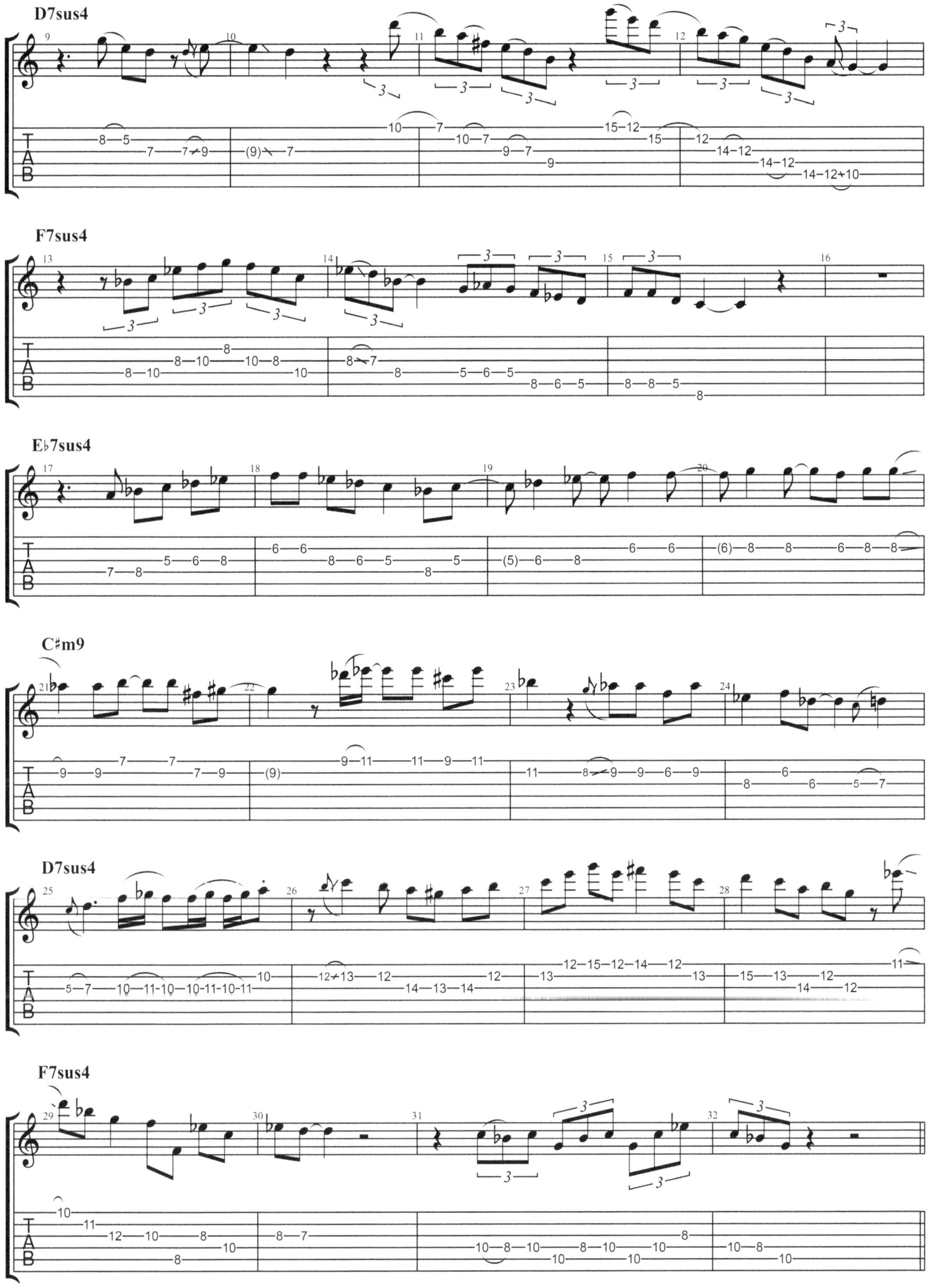
D7sus4
F7sus4
E♭7sus4
C♯m9
D7sus4
F7sus4

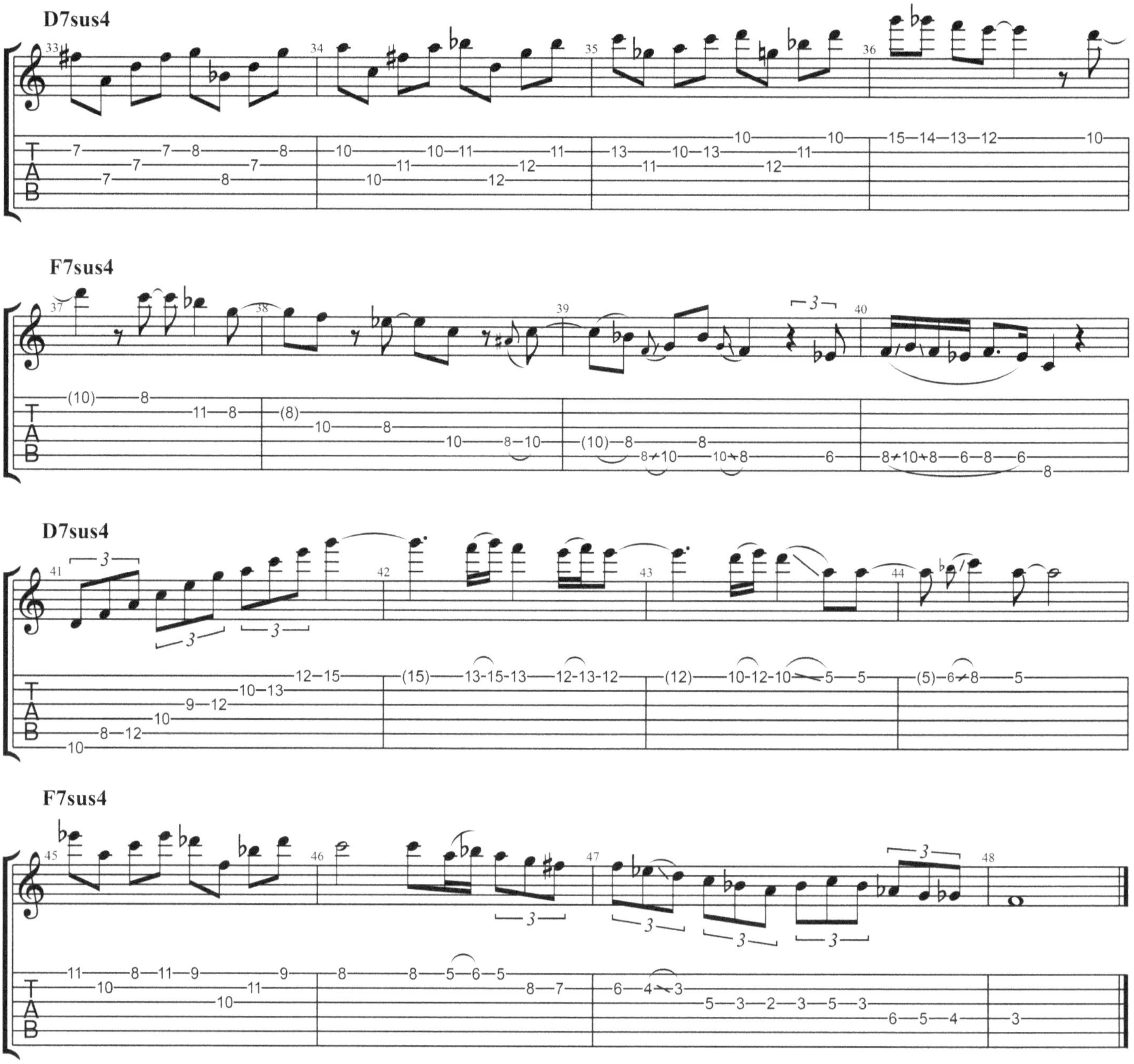
D7sus4
F7sus4
D7sus4
F7sus4

Conclusion – Taking These Ideas Forward

Throughout this book, we've explored a broad palette of modal soloing strategies designed to help you improvise with greater creativity, confidence, and melodic control. By moving beyond traditional chord-change thinking and embracing wider modal concepts, I hope you've begun to develop some tools to unlock new textures and moods in your playing.

We began by delving into the minor modal world of *So What* and *Impressions*, using the Dorian scale and its associated pentatonic variations to build strong, motif-led phrasing. We then expanded into hybrid pentatonics and melodic minor applications, discovering how modern players such as John Scofield, or legendary saxophonist Michael Brecker, derive intervallic, contemporary lines from these compact ideas.

As we explored dominant vamps and modal blues, we touched on Pat Martino's "minorization" approach by superimposing minor ideas a fifth above the root to access sophisticated sounds, as well as Lydian Dominant ideas and chromatic targeting techniques to bring a more modern harmonic edge.

The major 7 and major 7#11 chapter showed how relative minor pentatonics and Lydian or Melodic Minor options help to modernize our melodic vocabulary, while the 7sus4 chords chapter opened the door to triad pairs, hybrid pentatonics, and modal interchange as heard in *Maiden Voyage*.

Finally, the example solos demonstrated how these tools combine in musical, melodic contexts, and aimed to demonstrate that the goal of modal soloing is not theory for its own sake, but melody, narrative, and expression.

Next Steps for Your Playing

1. There is no substitute for *immersive listening*. Revisit the playlist from the introduction and listen to the work of Miles Davis, John Coltrane, Herbie Hancock, Wayne Shorter and McCoy Tyner. You must also listen to the work of Kurt Rosenwinkel, the godfather of modern jazz guitar, for his modal approach.

Listen out for and transcribe short motifs from their playing. Hearing how masters navigate static harmony will deepen your understanding and intuition for this music.

2. Practice your scales and modes over static chord vamps. Record some long loops and move from idea to idea. Focus on hearing each scale's *character notes*, such as the Dorian's 6th or the Lydian's #4. Hearing those character notes is more important than just visualizing shapes.

3. We all love to hear scale sequences in solos, but focus mostly on *developing motifs* rather than runs. Limiting yourself to using a small cell or triad pair, then developing it rhythmically and melodically over a vamp is a very fruitful exercise. Meaningful solos can grow out of such ideas, rather than playing pre-practiced patterns.

4. As you grow in confidence, trying *combining concepts*. Blend hybrid pentatonics with the Melodic Minor, or move between Lydian and Dorian shapes. The boundaries between modes are flexible, so feel free to experiment.

5. Whenever possible, *record your improvisation* using this book's backing tracks. Then listen back and "self-edit". Notice where your lines feel the most melodic, and where they sound mechanical or the phrasing is awkward. I know of no quicker way to refine your playing!

6. Finally, remember Martin Taylor's advice: no one goes home from a gig whistling the Phrygian Dominant! Technique and theory are only means of serving the music, so use them like the tools they are and keep melody first.

Above all, enjoy your playing and never allow it to stand still. Keep exploring!

www.ingramcontent.com/pod-product-compliance
Lightning Source LLC
Chambersburg PA
CBHW081434090426
42740CB00017B/3302